Copyright © 2015 James Connor | **connorfun.com**
All rights reserved. No parts of this book may be reproduced
in any form without written permission from the publisher.

This book is a work of humor meant solely for entertainment
purposes.
Every reasonable attempt has been made to identify owners of
copyright. Errors or omissions will be corrected in subsequent
editions.

Where specific company, product, and brand names are cited,
copyright and trademarks associated with these names are
property of their respective owners.

I0450520

Manufactured in space
All content and design by **connorfun.com**

This page is currently unavailable

CONTENTS

Check out the website for more cool stuff

www.connorfun.com

INTRODUCTION

'What is love' was the most searched question in Google in 2014. That asks for an explanation.

We already know that love is actually a powerful neurological condition like hunger or thirst, only more permanent. Our brain can release a whole set of chemicals: pheromones, dopamine, norepinephrine, serotine, oxytocin… However, from an evolutionary perspective, love is more like a survival tool.

At his best love, all love is a kind a passionate commitment that we nurture and develop, even though it usually arrives in our lives unbidden. That is why it is more than just a powerful feeling.

Love is the driver for all great stories.

But what do the people of the world really think about love?

In this book I tried to bring together all the best quotes/definitions about love that people have made during the years.

So I am sure after reading this book you will have a good understanding what LOVE really is! (And of course you will also have a good laugh sometimes…)

WTF IS LOVE

...

WHAT IS LOVE

People exploit you just for the fun of it.
Having no idea, how deeply it may effect
you..

———◦❦❧◦———

Love is friendship that has caught fire. It is
quiet understanding, mutual confidence,
sharing and forgiving. It is loyalty through
good and bad times. It settles for less than
perfection and makes allowances for human
weaknesses.

———◦❦❧◦———

Love is when the other person's happiness is
more important than your own.

———◦❦❧◦———

Love doesn't make the world go 'round. Love
is what makes the ride worthwhile.

———◦❦❧◦———

Love is composed of a single soul inhabiting
two bodies.

———◦❦❧◦———

I believe that imagination is stronger than knowledge. That myth is more potent than history. That dreams are more powerful than facts. That hope always triumphs over experience. That laughter is the only cure for grief. And I believe that love is stronger than death.

Love is when he gives you a piece of your soul, that you never knew was missing.

Love is the only force capable of transforming an enemy into friend.

The first duty of love is to listen.

Love is a force more formidable than any other. It is invisible - it cannot be seen or measured, yet it is powerful enough to transform you in a moment, and offer you more joy than any material possession could.

Love isn't something you find. Love is something that finds you.

Mama was my greatest teacher, a teacher of compassion, love and fearlessness. If love is sweet as a flower, then my mother is that sweet flower of love.

Love is the magician that pulls man out of his own hat.

Love is the joy of the good, the wonder of the wise, the amazement of the Gods.

We've got this gift of love, but love is like a precious plant. You can't just accept it and leave it in the cupboard or just think it's going to get on by itself. You've got to keep watering it. You've got to really look after it and nurture it.

Power is of two kinds. One is obtained by the fear of punishment and the other by acts of love. Power based on love is a thousand times more effective and permanent then the one derived from fear of punishment.

True love is eternal, infinite, and always like itself. It is equal and pure, without violent demonstrations: it is seen with white hairs and is always young in the heart.

Love is a game that two can play and both win.

Love is but the discovery of ourselves in others, and the delight in the recognition.

The story of life is quicker than the blink of an eye, the story of love is hello, goodbye.

Love is an emotion experienced by the many and enjoyed by the few.

Love is like a friendship caught on fire. In the beginning a flame, very pretty, often hot and fierce, but still only light and flickering. As love grows older, our hearts mature and our

love becomes as coals, deep-burning and
unquenchable.

———⁂———

Love is that condition in which the happiness
of another person is essential to your own...
Jealousy is a disease, love is a healthy
condition. The immature mind often mistakes
one for the other, or assumes that the greater
the love, the greater the jealousy.

———⁂———

The beginning of love is to let those we love
be perfectly themselves, and not to twist them
to fit our own image. Otherwise we love only
the reflection of ourselves we find in them.

———⁂———

To love is so startling it leaves little time for
anything else.

———⁂———

Love is like a beautiful flower which I may
not touch, but whose fragrance makes the
garden a place of delight just the same.

———⁂———

The beginning of love is to let those we love
be perfectly themselves, and not to twist them

to fit our own image. Otherwise we love only
the reflection of ourselves we find in them.

Where we love is home - home that our feet
may leave, but not our hearts.

Sex without love is a meaningless experience,
but as far as meaningless experiences go its
pretty damn good.

Love is always bestowed as a gift - freely,
willingly and without expectation. We don't
love to be loved; we love to love.

Music is love, love is music, music is life, and
I love my life. Thank you and good night.

Love is the flower you've got to let grow.

True love is not a strong, fiery, impetuous
passion. It is, on the contrary, an element calm
and deep. It looks beyond mere externals, and
is attracted by qualities alone. It is wise and

discriminating, and its devotion is real and abiding.

My brothers and sisters, true love is a reflection of the Savior's love. In December of each year we call it the Christmas spirit. You can hear it. You can see it. You can feel it.

Love does not begin and end the way we seem to think it does. Love is a battle, love is a war; love is a growing up.

True love is like ghosts, which everyone talks about and few have seen.

Love is the crowning grace of humanity, the holiest right of the soul, the golden link which binds us to duty and truth, the redeeming principle that chiefly reconciles the heart to life, and is prophetic of eternal good.

The secret to a happy marriage is if you can be at peace with someone within four walls, if you are content because the one you love is near to you, either upstairs or downstairs, or in the same room, and you feel that warmth that you don't find very often, then that is what love is all about.

———❦———

Love is a really scary thing, and you never know what's going to happen. It's one of the most beautiful things in life, but it's one of the most terrifying. It's worth the fear because you have more knowledge, experience, you learn from people, and you have memories.

———❦———

Love is the triumph of imagination over intelligence.

———❦———

Love is our true destiny. We do not find the meaning of life by ourselves alone - we find it with another.

———❦———

Love is never lost. If not reciprocated, it will flow back and soften and purify the heart.

———❦———

My friends, love is better than anger. Hope is better than fear. Optimism is better than despair. So let us be loving, hopeful and optimistic. And we'll change the world.

Love is a smoke made with the fume of sighs.

The art of love is largely the art of persistence.

Love is life. And if you miss love, you miss life.

Life without love is like a tree without blossoms or fruit.

Love many things, for therein lies the true strength, and whosoever loves much performs much, and can accomplish much, and what is done in love is done well.

We are born of love; Love is our mother.

Love is blind; friendship closes its eyes.

The romantic love we feel toward the opposite sex is probably one extra help from God to bring you together, but that's it. All the rest of it, the true love, is the test.

The art of love is largely the art of persistence.

Love is blind; friendship closes its eyes.

True love is selfless. It is prepared to sacrifice.

Even if a unity of faith is not possible, a unity of love is.

Love one another and help others to rise to the higher levels, simply by pouring out love. Love is infectious and the greatest healing energy.

We are born of love; Love is our mother.

Life without love is like a tree without blossoms or fruit.

Love is a fruit in season at all times, and within reach of every hand.

Love is something far more than desire for sexual intercourse; it is the principal means of escape from the loneliness which afflicts most men and women throughout the greater part of their lives.

Life is the flower for which love is the honey.

The richest love is that which submits to the arbitration of time.

When love is not madness, it is not love.

Love is being stupid together.

Being in love is the best feeling on the planet. I really believe that love makes the world go round.

Love is like a virus. It can happen to anybody at any time.

Love is not just tolerance. It's not just distant appreciation. It's a warm sense of, 'I am enjoying the fact that you are you.'

Love is of all passions the strongest, for it attacks simultaneously the head, the heart and the senses.

Since love grows within you, so beauty grows. For love is the beauty of the soul.

Love is the only reality and it is not a mere sentiment. It is the ultimate truth that lies at the heart of creation.

Miracles occur naturally as expressions of love. The real miracle is the love that inspires them. In this sense everything that comes from love is a miracle.

Love is so short, forgetting is so long.

I have a very strong feeling that the opposite of love is not hate - it's apathy. It's not giving a damn.

Love is the greatest gift that God has given us. It's free.

Love is the answer, and you know that for sure; Love is a flower, you've got to let it grow.

Love is like war: easy to begin but very hard to stop.

Miracles occur naturally as expressions of love. The real miracle is the love that inspires them. In this sense everything that comes from love is a miracle.

Absence from whom we love is worse than death, and frustrates hope severer than despair.

Love is so short, forgetting is so long.

Love is not only something you feel, it is something you do.

Falling in love is the best way to kill your heart because then it's not yours anymore. It's laid in a coffin, waiting to be cremated.

Love is of all passions the strongest, for it attacks simultaneously the head, the heart and the senses.

Even if a unity of faith is not possible, a unity of love is.

———— ❧❦❧ ————

Romantic love is mental illness. But it's a pleasurable one. It's a drug. It distorts reality, and that's the point of it. It would be impossible to fall in love with someone that you really saw.

———— ❧❦❧ ————

If love is the treasure, laughter is the key.

———— ❧❦❧ ————

Love is not just tolerance. It's not just distant appreciation. It's a warm sense of, 'I am enjoying the fact that you are you.'

———— ❧❦❧ ————

Love is space and time measured by the heart.

———— ❧❦❧ ————

I have a very strong feeling that the opposite of love is not hate - it's apathy. It's not giving a damn.

———— ❧❦❧ ————

Love is a strange emotion. It is ever evolving. Lust is transient. With time, one realizes that love and togetherness are two different things. Very few people are lucky enough to experience the two emotions simultaneously.

———⟨❈⟩———

Love is a sacred reserve of energy; it is like the blood of spiritual evolution.

———⟨❈⟩———

The best proof of love is trust.

———⟨❈⟩———

Love is the flower of life, and blossoms unexpectedly and without law, and must be plucked where it is found, and enjoyed for the brief hour of its duration.

———⟨❈⟩———

The garden of love is green without limit and yields many fruits other than sorrow or joy. Love is beyond either condition: without spring, without autumn, it is always fresh.

———⟨❈⟩———

Doing what you love is the cornerstone of having abundance in your life.

———⟨❈⟩———

The fact is that love is of two kinds, one which commands, and one which obeys. The two are quite distinct, and the passion to which the one gives rise is not the passion of the other.

———❦———

Love is flower like; Friendship is like a sheltering tree.

———❦———

Where love is concerned, too much is not even enough.

———❦———

With love, you should go ahead and take the risk of getting hurt because love is an amazing feeling.

———❦———

Love is a chain of love as nature is a chain of life.

———❦———

I think the perfection of love is that it's not perfect.

———❦———

Life is a game and true love is a trophy.

———❦———

Love is the greatest refreshment in life.

———✦❈✦———

Love is a trap. When it appears, we see only its light, not its shadows.

———✦❈✦———

Being in love is the only transcendent experience.

———✦❈✦———

Love is like the measles; we all have to go through it.

———✦❈✦———

Love is the great miracle cure. Loving ourselves works miracles in our lives.

———✦❈✦———

The giving of love is an education in itself.

———✦❈✦———

Doing what you love is the cornerstone of having abundance in your life.

———✦❈✦———

Love is when you meet someone who tells you something new about yourself.

Falling in love is the best way to kill your
heart because then it's not yours anymore. It's
laid in a coffin, waiting to be cremated.

Beauty, sweet love, is like the morning dew,
Whose short refresh upon tender green,
Cheers for a time, but till the sun doth show
And straight is gone, as it had never been.

Our first and last love is self-love.

Life is a game and true love is a trophy.

A friendship that like love is warm; A love
like friendship, steady.

Love is not only something you feel, it is
something you do.

Love is a canvas furnished by nature and
embroidered by imagination.

The loss of young first love is so painful that it borders on the ludicrous.

Love is flower like; Friendship is like a sheltering tree.

Love is the word used to label the sexual excitement of the young, the habituation of the middle-aged, and the mutual dependence of the old.

Love is a sacred reserve of energy; it is like the blood of spiritual evolution.

When love is at its best, one loves so much that he cannot forget.

With love, you should go ahead and take the risk of getting hurt because love is an amazing feeling.

The garden of love is green without limit and yields many fruits other than sorrow or joy. Love is beyond either condition: without spring, without autumn, it is always fresh.

Love is the flower of life, and blossoms unexpectedly and without law, and must be plucked where it is found, and enjoyed for the brief hour of its duration.

Mental prayer in my opinion is nothing else than an intimate sharing between friends; it means taking time frequently to be alone with Him who we know loves us. The important thing is not to think much but to love much and so do that which best stirs you to love. Love is not great delight but desire to please God in everything.

Love is a strange emotion. It is ever evolving. Lust is transient. With time, one realizes that love and togetherness are two different things. Very few people are lucky enough to experience the two emotions simultaneously.

Being in love is the only transcendent experience.

———⊱❈⊰———

A friendship that like love is warm; A love like friendship, steady.

———⊱❈⊰———

I enjoy writing about people falling in love, probably because I think the first time you fall in love is the first time that you have to figure out how you're going to orient your life. What are you going to value? What's going to be most important to you? And I think that's really interesting to write about.

———⊱❈⊰———

If fear is the great enemy of intimacy, love is its true friend.

———⊱❈⊰———

A lot of people say, 'Wow, you're a single father of twin boys, that's crazy!' Two toddlers can get hectic, but I wouldn't change it for anything. Every day they teach me different things. The love is there. When you have a two-year-old saying every other hour, 'Papi, te amo. Papi, I love you,' it can't get better.

———⊱❈⊰———

Where love rules, there is no will to power; and where power predominates, there love is lacking. The one is the shadow of the other.

———❈❈❈———

True love is quiescent, except in the nascent moments of true humility.

———❈❈❈———

Love is the attempt to form a friendship inspired by beauty.

———❈❈❈———

I think falling in love is always a surprise, right?

———❈❈❈———

You hear about quality time a lot but I really think that quantity time with a person is really what strengthens a relationship. That's when you really get to know somebody. You get to know their strengths and their weaknesses and that brings you closer. That's what 'Time Is Love' is all about.

———❈❈❈———

Whatever else is unsure in this stinking dunghill of a world a mother's love is not.

———❈❈❈———

For the most part, that message hasn't changed a lot over the years - love is still love, and heartbreak is still heartbreak.

Love is staying up all night with a sick child - or a healthy adult.

Love is a positive, symbiotic, reciprocal flow between two or more entities.

Love is like the measles; we all have to go through it.

Love is the silent saying and saying of a single name.

When love is at its best, one loves so much that he cannot forget.

Of all the nonsense written about love, none is more absurd than the notion that ideal love is selfless. To love is to see myself in you and to wish to celebrate myself with you. What I love is the embodiment of my values in another person. Love is an act of self-assertion, self-expression and a celebration of being alive.

———❦❦❦———

The loss of young first love is so painful that it borders on the ludicrous.

———❦❦❦———

You need a lot of luck to find people with whom you want to spend the rest of your life. Some people manage to find their soul mate. Others don't. I think love is like a lottery.

———❦❦❦———

Love is the hardest habit to break, and the most difficult to satisfy.

———❦❦❦———

Love is a gross exaggeration of the difference between one person and everybody else.

———❦❦❦———

If my love is without sacrifice, it is selfish. Such a love is barter, for there is exchange of love and devotion in return for something. It is conditional love.

———❦❦❦———

Pure love is a willingness to give without a thought of receiving anything in return.

—————⊱⋆⊰—————

Love consists in giving without getting in return; in giving what is not owed, what is not due the other. That's why true love is never based, as associations for utility or pleasure are, on a fair exchange.

—————⊱⋆⊰—————

The deep joy we take in the company of people with whom we have just recently fallen in love is undisguisable.

—————⊱⋆⊰—————

Love is an exploding cigar we willingly smoke.

—————⊱⋆⊰—————

The essence of romantic love is that wonderful beginning, after which sadness and impossibility may become the rule.

—————⊱⋆⊰—————

Look your best - who said love is blind?

—————⊱⋆⊰—————

Never pretend to a love which you do not actually feel, for love is not ours to command.

Ultimately love is everything.

'Back To Love' is a way of letting people know that sometimes you get caught up in trying to be successful in school or in your social life, and it's a reminder not to forget that each day people are getting older. Nobody is promised tomorrow, so we should make sure that we spend quality time with quality people.

Love is a springtime plant that perfumes everything with its hope, even the ruins to which it clings.

Love is always a leap into the unknown. You can try to control as many variables, and understand a situation as you can, but you're still jumping off a cliff and hoping that someone catches you.

Love is the great miracle cure. Loving
ourselves works miracles in our lives.

Unable are the loved to die, for love is
immortality.

Love is anterior to life, posterior to death,
initial of creation, and the exponent of breath.

The truth is that there is only one terminal
dignity - love. And the story of a love is not
important - what is important is that one is
capable of love. It is perhaps the only glimpse
we are permitted of eternity.

Falling in love is awesome, but I'm never
drawn to happy songs per se, so whenever
you sit down to write a heartbreak song and
you're happily in love, it's like, 'OK, now I
have to go back to a sad place to get
something good.'

I think tolerance and acceptance and love is
something that feeds every community.

If one is desperate for love, I suggest looking at one's friends and family and see if love is all around. If not, get a new set of friends, a new family.

To fear love is to fear life, and those who fear life are already three parts dead.

To fall in love is easy, even to remain in it is not difficult; our human loneliness is cause enough. But it is a hard quest worth making to find a comrade through whose steady presence one becomes steadily the person one desires to be.

Love is the only gold.

There are only really a few stories to tell in the end, and betrayal and the failure of love is one of those good stories to tell.

As for what concerns our relations with our fellow men, the anguish in our neighbor's soul must break all precept. All that we do is a means to an end, but love is an end in itself, because God is love.

———❦———

The whole idea of love is scary - so is being with someone for the rest of your life and being happy with them for the rest of your life. There's lots of research to suggest that, actually, love's not really that simple.

———❦———

Love is a better teacher than duty.

———❦———

A man in love is incomplete until he has married. Then he's finished.

———❦———

I understand now that the vulnerability I've always felt is the greatest strength a person can have. You can't experience life without feeling life. What I've learned is that being vulnerable to somebody you love is not a weakness, it's a strength.

———❦———

Love is an act of endless forgiveness, a tender look which becomes a habit.

———◈◈◈———

Love is a special word, and I use it only when I mean it. You say the word too much and it becomes cheap.

———◈◈◈———

A man without ambition is dead. A man with ambition but no love is dead. A man with ambition and love for his blessings here on earth is ever so alive.

———◈◈◈———

Love is like the wild rose-briar; Friendship like the holly-tree. The holly is dark when the rose-briar blooms, but which will bloom most constantly?

———◈◈◈———

Love is union with somebody, or something, outside oneself, under the condition of retaining the separateness and integrity of one's own self.

———◈◈◈———

Love is when the desire to be desired takes you so badly that you feel you could die of it.

Love is an endless mystery, for it has nothing else to explain it.

Love is the emotion that a woman feels always for a poodle dog and sometimes for a man.

Love is when you don't have to be with another person to touch their heart!

Love is not weakness. It is strong. Only the sacrament of marriage can contain it.

Love is the bond of perfection.

Love is what you've been through with somebody.

Romance is tempestuous. Love is calm.

Free love? as if love is anything but free. Man has bought brains, but all the millions in the world have failed to buy love.

Love is not love, without a violin playing goat.

Love rules the court, the camp, the grove, And men below, and saints above: For love is heaven, and heaven is love.

Love is the most terrible, and also the most generous of the passions; it is the only one which includes in its dreams the happiness of someone else.

Love is supreme and unconditional; like is nice but limited.

Love is moral even without legal marriage, but marriage is immoral without love.

Love is not to be purchased, and affection has no price.

Love is blind.

But love is really more of an interactive process. It's about what we do not just what we feel. It's a verb, not a noun.

Love is not a fire to be shut up in a soul. Everything betrays us: voice, silence, eyes; half-covered fires burn all the brighter.

The true treasure lies within. It is the underlying theme of the songs we sing, the shows we watch and the books we read. It is woven into the Psalms of the Bible, the ballads of the Beatles and practically every Bollywood film ever made. What is that treasure? Love. Love is the nature of the Divine.

Love is a serious mental disease.

Love is the child of illusion and the parent of disillusion.

———◈◆◈———

First love is a kind of vaccination which saves a man from catching the complaint the second time.

———◈◆◈———

Love is the one wild card.

———◈◆◈———

First love is first love, first marriage is first marriage, disappointment is disappointment.

———◈◆◈———

Love is a perky elf dancing a merry little jig and then suddenly he turns on you with a miniature machine gun.

———◈◆◈———

Real love is more than a physical feeling. If there's even the slightest doubt in your head about a guy, then forget about it. It's not real.

———◈◆◈———

Love is such a powerful subject matter because it comes in so many different shapes and sizes. It's about timing, fate, failure, redemption.

Sex without love is merely healthy exercise.

Love is a reciprocal torture.

The measure of a man is not how great his faith is, but how great his love is. We must not let government programs disconnect our souls from each other.

The story of a love is not important-what is important is that one is capable of love. It is perhaps the only glimpse we are permitted of eternity.

Loving can cost a lot but not loving always costs more, and those who fear to love often find that want of love is an emptiness that robs the joy from life.

On the last analysis, then, love is life. Love never faileth and life never faileth so long as there is love.

Courage is managing fear to accomplish what you want to accomplish. And it's a great demonstration of love. It's really what love is. It's finding areas in which other people are more important than you.

Being in love is the best thing in my life.

Mental prayer in my opinion is nothing else than an intimate sharing between friends; it means taking time frequently to be alone with Him who we know loves us. The important thing is not to think much but to love much and so do that which best stirs you to love. Love is not great delight but desire to please God in everything.

Any time not spent on love is wasted.

Love is what we were born with. Fear is what
we learned here.

———⊰❈⊱———

If you're lucky enough to have a pretty girl
love you and share herself and sleep with
you, make that your secret. The best way to
spoil love is by talking to too many people
about it.

———⊰❈⊱———

The fate of love is that it always seems too
little or too much.

———⊰❈⊱———

Love is the expression of one's values, the
greatest reward you can earn for the moral
qualities you have achieved in your character
and person, the emotional price paid by one
man for the joy he receives from the virtues of
another.

———⊰❈⊱———

Dare, dream, dance, smile, and sing loudly!
And have faith that love is an unstoppable
force!

———⊰❈⊱———

I believe in love at first sight, and I feel
sometimes you have to just be open to
whatever love is and let yourself fall.

———◦◦❊◦◦———

Mature love is composed and sustaining; a
celebration of commitment, companionship,
and trust.

———◦◦❊◦◦———

Lust is temporary, romance can be nice, but
love is the most important thing of all.
Because without love, lust and romance will
always be short-lived.

———◦◦❊◦◦———

Love is pure and true; love knows no gender.

———◦◦❊◦◦———

Love is a symbol of eternity. It wipes out all
sense of time, destroying all memory of a
beginning and all fear of an end.

———◦◦❊◦◦———

First love is only a little foolishness and a lot
of curiosity.

———◦◦❊◦◦———

Love is always open arms. If you close your arms about love you will find that you are left holding only yourself.

———❖❖❖❖———

Love is the affinity which links and draws together the elements of the world... Love, in fact, is the agent of universal synthesis.

———❖❖❖❖———

For love is immortality.

———❖❖❖❖———

Love is like the measles. The older you get it, the worse the attack.

———❖❖❖❖———

Falling in love is a chemical reaction. But it wears off in a year. That's why you need a strong line of communication... which includes laughter.

———❖❖❖❖———

Love is metaphysical gravity.

———❖❖❖❖———

Falling out of love is chiefly a matter of forgetting how charming someone is.

I have been astonished that men could die martyrs for religion - I have shuddered at it. I shudder no more - I could be martyred for my religion - Love is my religion - I could die for that.

When I hear other people's stories, I like to believe that they contribute to my 'Encyclopedia of Human Experience.' The stories I hear help me expand my definition of what love is, what pain feels like, what sacrifice means, what laughter can do.

Love is the ultimate outlaw. It just won't adhere to any rules. The most any of us can do is sign on as its accomplice.

Love is a piano dropped from a fourth story window, and you were in the wrong place at the wrong time.

Real love is the love that sometimes arises after sensual pleasure: if it does, it is immortal; the other kind inevitably goes stale, for it lies in mere fantasy.

Love is my religion - I could die for it.

Love is when each person is more concerned for the other than for one's self.

Lust is what keeps you wanting to do it even when you have no desire to be with each other. Love is what makes you want to be with each other even when you have no desire to do it.

Love is the best school, but the tuition is high and the homework can be painful.

Love possesses not nor will it be possessed, for love is sufficient unto love.

The flowering of love is meditation.

Love is the power to see similarity in the dissimilar.

———◆❄◆———

You don't know what unconditional love is. You may say you do, but if you don't have a child, you don't know what that is. But when you experience it, it is the most fulfilling ever.

———◆❄◆———

Love is much nicer to be in than an automobile accident, a tight girdle, a higher tax bracket or a holding pattern over Philadelphia.

———◆❄◆———

When we recognise the virtues, the talent, the beauty of Mother Earth, something is born in us, some kind of connection, love is born.

———◆❄◆———

Love is tested in so many ways. How do I articulate this? Two people are together. There are stakes, strife, struggles, all these things that make us fall for someone, love someone even more, leave someone.

———◆❄◆———

Love is about mutual respect, apart from attraction.

———❖❈❖———

I believe love just happens once. You can be mistaken, you can think you are in love, but after a while you discover that you're really not. Real love is different.

———❖❈❖———

The traditional family table is round. No corners. No sides. No head. No tail. Everything is smooth. The food is in the center, and each family member reaches over the same distance. Someone you love is next to you on each side, and no one is last or at the end. The person farthest away from you is also the person facing you.

———❖❈❖———

To be in love is merely to be in a state of perceptual anesthesia - to mistake an ordinary young woman for a goddess.

———❖❈❖———

If one of two lovers is loyal, and the other jealous and false, how may their friendship last, for Love is slain!

———❖❈❖———

Suffering passes, while love is eternal. That's a gift that you have received from God. Don't waste it.

The only true love is love at first sight; second sight dispels it.

Love is or it ain't. Thin love ain't love at all.

Romantic love is an addiction.

If a person loves only one other person and is indifferent to all others, his love is not love but a symbiotic attachment, or an enlarged egotism.

If love is the answer, could you please rephrase the question?

Love is all we have, the only way that each can help the other.

Love is suffering. One side always loves more.

Just as love is an orientation which refers to all objects and is incompatible with the restriction to one object, so is reason a human faculty which must embrace the whole of the world with which man is confronted.

Young love is a flame; very pretty, often very hot and fierce, but still only light and flickering. The love of the older and disciplined heart is as coals, deep-burning, unquenchable.

Love is the delightful interval between meeting a beautiful girl and discovering that she looks like a haddock.

Love is energy of life.

Love is friendship set on fire.

Fantasy love is much better than reality love.

Love is very dangerous if you just have love
and don't have the ability to be lovable.

———❖❖❖———

To fall in love is to create a religion that has a
fallible god.

———❖❖❖———

Everything that I love is behind those gates.
We have elephants, and giraffes, and
crocodiles, and every kind of tigers and lions.
And - and we have bus loads of kids, who
don't get to see those things. They come up
sick children, and enjoy it.

———❖❖❖———

When you have a baby, love is automatic,
when you get married, love is earned.

———❖❖❖———

A major part of love is commitment. If we are
committed to someone, if I'm committed to
loving you, then it's not possible for me to 'fall
out of love.'

———❖❖❖———

Being young and female in America, you watch a lot of T.V., and you grow up on false images of what love truly is. We think the man with the best rap will protect and save us, about it's not usually that way. Then you learn love is something deeper and purer in form.

———

Love is simply the name for the desire and the pursuit of the whole.

———

Looking for love is tricky business, like whipping a carousel horse.

———

Love is the most important thing in the world. Hate, we should remove from the dictionary.

———

Salvation and Christ's love is a gift. You don't earn it. You've got to receive that gift.

———

Love is only a dirty trick played on us to achieve continuation of the species.

———

Of all forms of caution, caution in love is perhaps the most fatal to true happiness.

———⋈⊰❈⊱⋈———

Love is never defeated, and I could add, the history of Ireland proves it.

———⋈⊰❈⊱⋈———

Love is the river of life in the world.

———⋈⊰❈⊱⋈———

Love is always being given where it is not required.

———⋈⊰❈⊱⋈———

I argue thee that love is life. And life hath immortality.

———⋈⊰❈⊱⋈———

Love is a mutual self-giving which ends in self-recovery.

———⋈⊰❈⊱⋈———

Infinite love is the only truth. Everything else is illusion.

———⋈⊰❈⊱⋈———

Love is an attempt at penetrating another being, but it can only succeed if the surrender is mutual.

The highest function of love is that it makes the loved one a unique and irreplacable being.

There is a physical relationship with a woman that you don't have with anybody else, but that's not about love. Love is a spiritual thing.

Poets are the only people to whom love is not only a crucial, but an indispensable experience, which entitles them to mistake it for a universal one.

Falling out of love is very enlightening. For a short while you see the world with new eyes.

The beginning of love is a horror of emptiness.

To enlarge or illustrate this power and effect
of love is to set a candle in the sun.

———❦❦❦———

The concept of romantic love affords a means
of emotional manipulation which the male is
free to exploit, since love is the only
circumstance in which the female is
(ideologically) pardoned for sexual activity.

———❦❦❦———

Love is the most difficult and dangerous form
of courage. Courage is the most desperate,
admirable and noble kind of love.

———❦❦❦———

There will always be crazy things that happen
in our lives, but love is the central connector.
If we commit to love and partnership, the
other stuff doesn't matter.

———❦❦❦———

The beauty we love is very silent. It smiles
softly to itself, but never speaks.

———❦❦❦———

Love proves itself by deeds, so how am I to
show my love? Great deeds are forbidden me.
The only way I can prove my love is by

scattering flowers, and these flowers are every little sacrifice, every glance and word, and the doing of the least actions for love.

Love is the outreach of self toward completion.

Love is rarer than genius itself. And friendship is rarer than love.

The concept of romantic love affords a means of emotional manipulation which the male is free to exploit, since love is the only circumstance in which the female is (ideologically) pardoned for sexual activity.

Love is the strongest and most fragile thing we have in life.

God makes it really clear that society and civilization is really held together by the glue of families... When a man and a woman come together and say 'I do,' they are committing for a lifetime to love each other and to model

what love is and what forgiveness is and what
joy is to their kids.

The beauty we love is very silent. It smiles
softly to itself, but never speaks.

Love proves itself by deeds, so how am I to
show my love? Great deeds are forbidden me.
The only way I can prove my love is by
scattering flowers, and these flowers are every
little sacrifice, every glance and word, and the
doing of the least actions for love.

Where love is, there God is also.

Love is trembling happiness.

Love grows by giving. The love we give away
is the only love we keep. The only way to
retain love is to give it away.

Love is the river of life in the world.

Love is a fire. But whether it is going to warm
your hearth or burn down your house, you
can never tell.

Love is not a feeling of happiness. Love is a
willingness to sacrifice.

Love is really the only thing we can possess,
keep with us, and take with us.

To love is to admire with the heart; to admire
is to love with the mind.

Love is not enough. It must be the foundation,
the cornerstone - but not the complete
structure. It is much too pliable, too yielding.

Power, after love, is the first source of
happiness.

Love is life's end, but never ending. Love is life's wealth, never spent, but ever spending. Love's life's reward, rewarded in rewarding.

———◆⬦◆———

Loving can cost a lot but not loving always costs more, and those who fear to love often find that want of love is an emptiness that robs the joy from life.

———◆⬦◆———

Love is one of my main inspirations.

———◆⬦◆———

Love is the force that ignites the spirit and binds teams together.

———◆⬦◆———

Love is three quarters curiosity.

———◆⬦◆———

Love is all you need.

———◆⬦◆———

Love is a state of Being. Your love is not outside; it is deep within you. You can never lose it, and it cannot leave you. It is not dependent on some other body, some external form.

The thing, when you're down two sets to love, is to stay calm, even though it's hard, because people are freaking out, people are worried for you.

Love is a portion of the soul itself, and it is of the same nature as the celestial breathing of the atmosphere of paradise.

The most powerful symptom of love is a tenderness which becomes at times almost insupportable.

Love is an emotion that is based on an opinion of women that is impossible for those who have had any experience with them.

Love is the only game that is not called on account of darkness.

Life is pain and the enjoyment of love is an anesthetic.

Family love is messy, clinging, and of an annoying and repetitive pattern, like bad wallpaper.

Love is a game in which one always cheats.

Love is easy, and I love writing. You can't resist love. You get an idea, someone says something, and you're in love.

Love is the answer to everything. It's the only reason to do anything. If you don't write stories you love, you'll never make it. If you don't write stories that other people love, you'll never make it.

We really have to understand the person we want to love. If our love is only a will to possess, it is not love. If we only think of ourselves, if we know only our own needs and ignore the needs of the other person, we cannot love.

Like the measles, love is most dangerous
when it comes late in life.

———⪦⪧———

Love is the hardest lesson in Christianity; but,
for that reason, it should be most our care to
learn it.

———⪦⪧———

Love is that splendid triggering of human
vitality the supreme activity which nature
affords anyone for going out of himself
toward someone else.

———⪦⪧———

As love without esteem is capricious and
volatile; esteem without love is languid and
cold.

———⪦⪧———

Love is all around us all the time. Love is the
ethers that we swim in. Love is the amniotic
fluid of the soul.

———⪦⪧———

I would rather live and love where death is
king than have eternal life where love is not.

———⪦⪧———

Love is the difficult realization that something other than oneself is real.

Love is a binding force, by which another is joined to me and cherished by myself.

Love is unknown. To open the heart in trust is unknown. They say love hurts. It doesn't have to.

Love is the cheapest of religions.

Love is a promise delivered already broken.

I think that making love is the best form of exercise.

Sometimes love is stronger than a man's convictions.

Love is the best thing in the world, and the thing that lives the longest.

I have rules for a lot of areas of my life. Love is not going to be one of them.

Love is a snowmobile racing across the tundra and then suddenly it flips over, pinning you underneath. At night, the ice weasels come.

Who would give a law to lovers? Love is unto itself a higher law.

Sex is like washing your face - just something you do because you have to. Sex without love is absolutely ridiculous. Sex follows love, it never precedes it.

How do you know love is gone? If you said that you would be there at seven and you get there by nine, and he or she has not called the police yet - it's gone.

Power, after love, is the first source of happiness.

———❧❦❧———

Love is, above all, the gift of oneself.

———❧❦❧———

All love is vanquished by a succeeding love.

———❧❦❧———

Love is like a faucet, it turns off and on.

———❧❦❧———

Love is the total absence of fear. Love asks no questions. Its natural state is one of extension and expansion, not comparison and measurement.

———❧❦❧———

Love is an energy which exists of itself. It is its own value.

———❧❦❧———

Your kids are happy if you're happy. And if your love is happy, then everything works. I think a lot of people think once the children are there, it's all about the children. But you can't forget about your best friend, your lover, your husband.

We love even when our love is not requited.

Real love is a permanently self-enlarging experience.

Clearly, love is love, between a man and a woman, a woman and a man, a woman and a woman and a man and a man.

Love is the opener as well as closer of eyes.

To be loved is a strength. To love is a weakness.

When love is gone, there's always justice. And when justice is gone, there's always force. And when force is gone, there's always Mom. Hi, Mom!

My definition of love is being full. Complete. It makes everything lighter. Beauty is

something you see. Love is something you
feel.

Love is not as important as good health. You
cannot be in love if you're not healthy. You
can't appreciate it.

It has ever been since time began, and ever
will be, till time lose breath, that love is a
mood - no more - to man, and love to a
woman is life or death.

Love is a thing that is full of cares and fears.

Love is seeing without eyes, hearing without
ears; hatred is nothing.

As to the deceit perpetrated upon women, let
it pass, for, when love is in the way, men and
women as a general rule dupe each other.

Love is an interesting thing.

Love is a given, hatred is acquired.

Nowadays love is a matter of chance, matrimony a matter of money and divorce a matter of course.

When love is suppressed hate takes its place.

Love is three quarters curiosity.

Love is a tyrant sparing none.

Love is like an hourglass, with the heart filling up as the brain empties.

Love is free; to promise for ever to love the same woman is not less absurd than to promise to believe the same creed; such a vow in both cases excludes us from all inquiry.

Love is a state of Being. Your love is not outside; it is deep within you. You can never lose it, and it cannot leave you. It is not dependent on some other body, some external form.

———⊰❈⊱———

At first I assumed hate was the opposite of love. But it isn't. The opposite of love is indifference.

———⊰❈⊱———

Love is the ultimate expression of the will to live.

———⊰❈⊱———

There is no fear when you choose love. The more you choose love, the more love is in your life. It gets easier and easier.

———⊰❈⊱———

Resignation, not mystic, not detached, but resignation open-eyed, conscious, and informed by love, is the only one of our feelings for which it is impossible to become a sham.

———⊰❈⊱———

Making love is like hitting a baseball. You just gotta relax and concentrate.

———✦✧❈✧✦———

Love is 2 minutes and 52 seconds of squelching noises.

———✦✧❈✧✦———

Love is not in our choice but in our fate.

———✦✧❈✧✦———

But groundless hope, like unconditional love, is the only kind worth having.

———✦✧❈✧✦———

With compassion you can die for other people, like the mother who can die for her child. You have the courage to say it because you are not afraid of losing anything, because you know that understanding and love is the foundation of happiness. But if you have fear of losing your status, your position, you will not have the courage to do it.

———✦✧❈✧✦———

The little trouble in the world that is not due to love is due to friendship.

———✦✧❈✧✦———

The way of peace is the way of love. Love is the greatest power on earth. It conquers all things.

World's use is cold, world's love is vain, world's cruelty is bitter bane; but is not the fruit of pain.

Love is a positive effect. Love can never have a negative effect, only a positive effect.

I believe in feeling connected. Love is something that grows, that comes from nourishment; it builds. But there is a great feeling that happens, that is telling you, I don't want to leave this room!

There's no text that can replace a loving touch when someone we love is hurting.

Normally, when someone we love is turning away from a struggle, we self-protect by also turning away. That's definitely my first response. I think change is more likely to happen if both partners have common language and a shared lens to see problems.

Every woman's path is difficult, and many mothers were as equipped to raise children as wire monkey mothers. I say that without judgment: It is, sadly, true. An unhealthy mother's love is withering.

Love is an indescribable sensation - perhaps a conviction, a sense of certitude.

Normally, when someone we love is turning away from a struggle, we self-protect by also turning away. That's definitely my first response. I think change is more likely to happen if both partners have common language and a shared lens to see problems.

Every woman's path is difficult, and many mothers were as equipped to raise children as wire monkey mothers. I say that without judgment: It is, sadly, true. An unhealthy mother's love is withering.

Love is an indescribable sensation - perhaps a conviction, a sense of certitude.

———❦———

Jealousy would be far less torturous if we understood that love is a passion entirely unrelated to our merits.

———❦———

Love is more powerful than kicking ass.

———❦———

Life is suffering. We have desires and expectations and egos, and we compare the reality we have, which is miraculous and wondrous, with this reality we desire. That somehow distances us from actually taking part fully with the reality we do have, and that creates suffering. For me, the thing that I love is that it's all about the present moment.

———❦———

Love is the only wealth that man absolutely needs. Love is the only wealth that God precisely is.

———❦———

The Dalai Lama said that he thinks mother's love is the best symbol for love and compassion, because it is totally disinterested.

———⊰⊱———

I might run from her for a thousand years and she is still my baby child. Our love is so furious that we burn each other out.

———⊰⊱———

I'm going to be a strict mum. I know that love is the most important thing - you've got to have lots of kisses and cuddles - but you also need to mix it with discipline or you'll be in a heap of trouble.

———⊰⊱———

Divorce can be crazy. Man, if you're happy... Love is a beast, man. Hold on. Be prepared for any way it may go, and be honest.

———⊰⊱———

When love is pure, it has the power to conquer. Lover and beloved conquer each other by their affection. The source, the essence, the fullest manifestation of love's conquering power is the love of the soul for the supreme soul, or God.

———⊰⊱———

Sometimes you resent the people you love and need the most. Love is so fascinating in all its forms, and I think everyone who has ever been a mother will relate to this.

———◦⊰❈⊱◦———

Religion is faith. Faith is belief without evidence. Belief without evidence cannot be shared. Faith is a feeling. Love is also a feeling, but love makes no universal claims. Love is pure.

———◦⊰❈⊱◦———

The reason you take antidepressants is to feel calm. And romantic love is not calm - it's elation, it's mood swings, and you're killing all that when you take the drug.

———◦⊰❈⊱◦———

Rekindled love is generally short-term.

———◦⊰❈⊱◦———

To be loved is important as is having a sense of accomplishment but to love is equally important in life especially when it is combined with taking action to do something for someone else to make their life better.

———◦⊰❈⊱◦———

I like to believe that love is a reciprocal thing, that it can't really be felt, truly, by one.

'Yes' is the mother of all positive words, next to 'love.' Maybe 'love' is the father of all positive words.

I believe eating well, and with people you love, is about feeding your body, heart, and soul - I used juicing to ensure I covered my nutritional bases every day, and as a tool to restore inner balance if my body needed a break from too much indulgence.

Whether it's a canvas tote or Givenchy, a day bag you love is essential. It doesn't have to be a fashion It bag of the season, either.

The jazz I love is sweet and pure with raw elements, which is exactly what the good hip-hop is doing now.

I still believe that love is the most powerful force in the world, even though I am yet to experience it fully.

You think you know what love is - until you have a child and discover that unconditional mother love.

Real love is a pilgrimage. It happens when there is no strategy, but it is very rare because most people are strategists.

Love is a deception and a trap. Love is as big a myth that God sits with his flowing white beard in a throne and looks at us.

As far as love is concerned, possession, power, fusion and disenchantment are the Four Horsemen of the Apocalypse.

Falling out of love is like losing weight. It's a lot easier putting it on than taking it off.

Life is the first gift, love is the second, and understanding the third.

———◦◦◦———

The only thing I really love is Fiji water. That's like the only crazy request - I don't like any other water.

———◦◦◦———

I mean, if you turn on the radio, love is 90 percent of the music.

———◦◦◦———

Harmony is pure love, for love is complete agreement.

———◦◦◦———

Love means that everything is right with the world. Love and only love. Love means that you are content within your own heart and in the presence of the person that you love, who fills your day and makes you stronger and wiser, and gives you the confidence to go out into the world. Love is just the most beautiful, joyous feeling.

———◦◦◦———

I don't think love is a tricky issue at all. Love is best understood when we share: Share time, energy, food, resources, insights, information, whatever. It's usually thought of as something that exists between two people, but that's just because it's easier to see and feel in the space between them. Each person is sharing a lot with the other.

Craziest thing I've done for love is getting married. I think it's crazy. I think it's crazy, crazy, crazy. I'm never going to say I wouldn't do it again but I have to make sure it's love and not settling for the 'I have to do this by a certain age,' which is kind of what I did.

My first love is art, and I see a lot of things in an artistic way.

However it is debased or misinterpreted, love is a redemptive feature. To focus on one individual so that their desires become superior to yours is a very cleansing experience.

It would appear that love is dead. Or very likely in a bad way.

To me, a forever love is a bond that can't be broken.

Love is a strange master, and human nature is still stranger.

I've really learned a lot, really learned a lot, love is like a stove, burns you when it's hot.

Before I had my child, I thought I knew all the boundaries of myself, that I understood the limits of my heart. It's extraordinary to have all those limits thrown out, to realize your love is inexhaustible.

Love is an attempt to change a piece of a dream world into reality.

Love is the expansion of two natures in such fashion that each include the other, each is enriched by the other.

Sensuality without love is a sin; love without sensuality is worse than a sin.

Love is such a confusing word. You think I'm joking but I'm not.

I haven't traveled in Africa nearly as much as I'd like to. I've been there a few times, and I'd like to learn more about the various cultures in Africa. But that's the basis point of where all of the music that I love is based upon, from Africa to Cuba to Puerto Rico to South America.

Go to the truth beyond the mind. Love is the bridge.

Falling in love is a chemical reaction. But it wears off in a year.

Making love is, simply put, poetry in motion.

I found my love when I was 17-years-old and my love is one hundred percent honest. We've never had any ugly, rocky things to overcome.

———❦———

Maharaj-ji, in my first darshan, my first meeting with him, showed me his powers. At that point I was impressed with the power. But subsequently, I realized that it was really his love that pulled me in. His love is unconditional love.

———❦———

Love is as strict as acting. If you want to love somebody, stand there and do it. If you don't, don't. There are no other choices.

———❦———

Love is higher than the Highest. Love is greater than the Greatest. Yea, it is in a certain sense greater than God; while yet, in the highest sense of all, God is Love, and Love is God. Love being the highest principle is the virtue of all virtues; from whence they flow forth.

———❦———

I feel like love is the thing we were created for, yet it's the place we struggle the most.

Being in love is not cool!

Everybody says love is about finding the person who is right for me and then everything will be fine. But it's not like that. It involves work. An old man tells you this!

The way you give love is the most profoundly human part of you. When people say it's ugly or a perversion or an abomination, they're attacking the center of your being.

Love is mutually feeding each other, not one living on another like a ghoul.

Love is so holy, so confusing. It makes a man anxious, tormented. Love, how can I define it?

Marrying to increase love is like gaming to become rich; alas, you only lose what little stock you had before.

I've never believed much in that holding hands kind of love. I've always thought that love is about two different personalities trying to confront life, trying to make sense of their responsibilities, to themselves, to each other, and to the wider society.

———⋙✦⋘———

My pure love is playing music.

———⋙✦⋘———

My first love is writing and producing. So I sometimes put my own stuff off to work on other people's projects.

———⋙✦⋘———

Love is the one emotion actors allow themselves to believe.

———⋙✦⋘———

Human love is often but the encounter of two weaknesses.

———⋙✦⋘———

The one snack I really love is YoCrunch yogurt. It's like an apple pie in a cup! You have your apples on the bottom, your yogurt in the middle, and piecrust crumbs on top.

———⋙✦⋘———

When love is absent, then there is fear, and in my opinion you should lead your entire life through love.

It has been said that love is a function of communication. I believe that to be true. I believe, by extension, that human understanding is a function of communication. And the better human beings understand one another, the higher the level of functioning.

Love is the last relay and ultimate outposts of eternity.

To tell you the truth, in my work, love is always in opposition to the elements. It creates dilemmas. It brings in suffering. We can't live with it, and we can't live without it. You'll rarely find a happy ending in my work.

I have the soundtrack for 'A Clockwork Orange,' which is kind of cool. I guess I don't really end up buying a lot of modern soundtracks. Another soundtrack I love is

from a French movie called 'Betty Blue.' it has
some really melancholy piano work.

———⋙✦⋘———

I was seeking a real love, a real deal, and I
have been seeking it for a lot of years. And in
that seeking, I found that God's love is real.

———⋙✦⋘———

Compatibility is weird. Love is confusing.
Love is one wild beast.

———⋙✦⋘———

Love is such an objective thing. I mean, I can
say I love my family, or I love my Diet Coke.
So I guess, in different ways, yeah, I do
believe in love.

———⋙✦⋘———

Love is such an objective thing. I mean, I can
say I love my family, or I love my Diet Coke.
So I guess, in different ways, yeah, I do
believe in love.

———⋙✦⋘———

Love is a great emotion, but I believe it's not
just about romance; it could be love for
nature, people, for relationships.

———⋙✦⋘———

My true love is with amateur wrestlin;, that's where I was born. I've always wanted to wrestle.

Anyone who thinks they can write the perfect comedy that everyone will love is a fool. I can only write what I think is funny and hope that there is a likeminded audience out there.

What I love is Mexican hot chocolate, like a spicy hot chocolate - adding cayenne pepper to the Hershey's cocoa and making a spicy-sweet treat.

Thy love is singular when all thy delight is in Jesus Christ and in no other thing finds joy and comfort.

I think the kind of unexpected I really love is when you open books and the actual way of writing is different and interesting. Like reading Virginia Woolf for the first time or Lawrence Durrell for the first time.

I believe love is the most powerful energy we have in this life. Everything is about love.

The way I see it, love is an amusement park, and food its souvenir.

From the time you are a tiny baby, a parent's love is usually unconditional. Whatever you do, your parents think you are the tops, but when their memory goes, you stop recouping the love you've put in.

Human beings are very complex creatures. This desire, this greed, this love is very complex.

Love is boundary-less.

My true love is history, but I didn't know how I could make a living at it.

My mother keeps things in perspective for me. She makes me realize that the acting I do

and love is no more important than what one
of my brothers does-he works in a shoe repair
shop. If my career ever tapers off, I'll go to
college.

———◦◦❈◦◦———

To me, spending your life doing what you
love is a gift. Everyone enjoys different walks
of life, so find what you love to do and try to
make a living at it.

———◦◦❈◦◦———

What I love is a good role. In the theatre, there
is just a canon of extraordinary roles, the
quality of character is amazing, but I also love
working in front of a camera. It was the first
one for me; as a kid I was in front of a camera.
I feel at home.

———◦◦❈◦◦———

Classic romantic love is an emotional
attraction between two individuals in which
they may share a heightened awareness of
mutual adoration. Erotic love, traditionally,
has been described as shared sexual
attraction.

———◦◦❈◦◦———

And love is love in beggars and in kings.

I know, being a father myself, what my interpretation of true love is, or the essence of love, and you can apply it to other things besides human beings.

Finding love is a fixation now, and that's because although romantic love can sometimes cause a lot of suffering, it can also give people peaks of happiness that come very close to our ideal of 'the happy state.'

For me, love is not about froufrou New Age-ism. It's about a way of living and honoring the interconnectedness of life and accepting our responsibility and our power to change the world for the better.

To be deeply in love is, of course, a great liberating force.

Love is the substance of all life. Everything is connected in love, absolutely everything.

Love is the bond between men, the way to teach and the center of the world.

I would have to say the person with whom I am most in love is definitely my son, Everly Bear. Although I'm his dad, I'm also his friend.

Love means that everything is right with the world. Love and only love. Love means that you are content within your own heart and in the presence of the person that you love, who fills your day and makes you stronger and wiser, and gives you the confidence to go out into the world. Love is just the most beautiful, joyous feeling.

Love is a sickness full of woes, All remedies refusing; A plant that with most cutting grows, Most barren with best using.

You may not be able to help whom you are attracted to, but you can choose to whom you love and how. That is to say that love is a commitment that your heart and your mind make. It is an active and ever-evolving process, a conscious choice that takes effort and maintenance.

To fail to love is not to exist at all.

The truth about love is that you don't always fall in love with whom you are supposed to fall in love with. Love just hits you. It is a transcendent thing. Sometimes it is your best friend's husband and sometimes it's your father. It's weird. But that's a fact of life.

To love one person with a private love is poor and miserable: to love all is glorious.

Love is the most ferocious and strongest force on the planet.

It's one of the most beautiful things in the world, to go off and make a film. At the heart of it, making a film - it's pretend. It's a silly thing to do. But it can be important, and to have that experience with people you love is one of the best things you can do.

Love is so simple.

As an American, and especially as a Christian, I am convinced that a love for our own people is not a bad thing, but love doesn't stop at borders. Love is infinitely boundless and all about holy trespassing and offensive friendships.

I never looked at basketball as work. I always enjoyed it as my hobby. I loved it. Once that love is gone, and I'm tired of working out every day and doing all the stuff to get me ready for games, and I'm tired of lifting and conditioning and doing all that other stuff around it, and I'd rather stay in bed, then it's time to go.

Young love is wild and outrageous, laughing at moderation and blinding us to common sense.

You know how big love is? Love is big. love can hold anger; love can even hold hatred.

To love is to act.

Love is a choice you make from moment to moment.

Love is the intuitive knowledge of our hearts.

Love is a great beautifier.

Love is only one of many passions.

Youth is not enough. And love is not enough. And success is not enough. And, if we could achieve it, enough would not be enough.

Let none think to fly the danger for soon or late love is his own avenger.

Love is the wisdom of the fool and the folly of the wise.

Love is said to be blind, but I know some fellows in love who can see twice as much in their sweethearts as I do.

My favorite thing in life is writing about life, specifically the parts of life concerning love. Because, as far as I'm concerned, love is absolutely everything.

Oh, love is real enough; you will find it someday, but it has one archenemy - and that is life.

Love is a kind of warfare.

Love is full of anxious fears.

The only way to real mature love is to get past the tropes of what we consider 'romance.'

Love is an interesting thing. Perhaps I've never been in love before - I don't really know? I think I have. I guess it's subjective in that way.

Love is a credulous thing.

Love is the strange bewilderment that overtakes one person on account of another person.

You study, you learn, but you guard the original naivete. It has to be within you, as desire for drink is within the drunkard or love is within the lover.

Love is a hole in the heart.

Whoever said love is blind is dead wrong. Love is the only thing that lets us see each other with the remotest accuracy.

Love is never wrong.

———·❦·———

If a person loves only one other person, and is indifferent to his fellow men, his love is not love but a symbiotic attachment, or an enlarged egotism.

———·❦·———

Everyone admits that love is wonderful and necessary, yet no one agrees on just what it is.

———·❦·———

I'd rather talk to people about their personal spiritual practices or what they believe love is. I'm born to do that. Could I enter into the political realm and dive into that? Sure, but I don't think I would want to do that.

———·❦·———

Oh, it is wonderful to know that our Heavenly Father loves us - even with all our flaws! His love is such that even should we give up on ourselves, He never will.

———·❦·———

It's very easy to fall in love when things are great, but the way to really fall in love is when things aren't great.

Love is more pleasant than marriage for the same reason that novels are more amusing than history.

Love is the capacity to take care, to protect, to nourish.

The reality is that we communicate with every part of our being, and there are times when we must use it all. When someone needs us, he or she needs all of us. There's no text that can replace a loving touch when someone we love is hurting.

Love is the whole history of a woman's life, it is but an episode in a man's.

I grew up watching MTV, when Journey was huge, when Pat Benatar had 'Love Is a Battlefield,' and my friends and I used to cut school to watch this woman in the video. We loved Pat Benatar.

Love is not an emotion; it is a drive.

———⟡⟡⟡———

Love is stronger than justice.

———⟡⟡⟡———

Love is not a volunteer thing.

———⟡⟡⟡———

Freud's view is that all love is sexual in its
origin or its basis. Even those loves which do
not appear to be sexual or erotic have a sexual
root or core. They are all sublimations of the
sexual instinct.

———⟡⟡⟡———

All is amiss. Love is dying, faith's defying,
heart's denying.

———⟡⟡⟡———

The Divine of the Lord in heaven is love, for
the reason that love is receptive of all things
of heaven, such as peace, intelligence, wisdom
and happiness.

———⟡⟡⟡———

Love is so much better when you're not
married.

Love is the funeral of hearts.

Love is the same as like except you feel sexier.

Hope is the most exciting thing in life, and if

---

you honestly believe that love is out there, it will come. And even if it doesn't come straight away, there is still that chance all through your life that it will.

Love is made by two people, in different kinds of solitude. It can be in a crowd, but in an oblivious crowd.

Love is cheap. You can buy it anywhere. Lives are cheap. It's money that's dear. You have to work days and sit up nights thinking how to make money.

Car love is the sound of a throaty V-8 rumbling and revving, the acceleration throwing you back in the seat - especially when you get on a beautiful, winding road and the light's dappling through the trees.

Love is sacrifice.

I think love is a really hard thing to define. I think it's multifaceted.

Book love... is your pass to the greatest, the purest, and the most perfect pleasure that God has prepared for His creatures.

To really understand what love is, you've kinda got to dig down deeper than just how you feel at the moment.

When I wrote songs like 'Everyone I Love is Dead,' I never thought about how I was going to execute them live.

Love is the motivating principle by which the Lord leads us along the way towards becoming like Him, our perfect example. Our way of life, hour by hour, must be filled with the love of God and love for others. There is no surprise in that, since the Lord proclaimed those as the first and great commandments.

The thing I love is that my home life hasn't changed. I still help out with the garbage. I still help out with the lawn.

I think being a parent is knowing how to love. Sometimes love is discipline, sometimes it's humor, sometimes it's listening.

Love is like any other luxury. You have no right to it unless you can afford it.

People marry for a variety of reasons and with varying results. But to marry for love is to invite inevitable tragedy.

I like all of the early relationship strips that were collected in 'Love Is Hell,' where I pretended to be an expert in relationships and did comics like 'The Nine Types of Boyfriends,' 'Sixteen Ways to End a Relationship,' 'Twenty-Four Things Not to Say in Bed,' and other arbitrarily numbered lists.

Love is always a stranger in the house of avarice.

Love can never make you weak, and love is not restricted to opposite sex. I love my parents, I love my animals, and I love my profession.

Love is a very powerful emotion and when a break-up is unexpected, it's very hard to get over.

Every one of us, no matter how damaged or abnormal or shut down, we're all looking for love. Every person needs love in this world, but our views on what love is vary enormously.

Love is blind. My politics has been, too. I think you can fall in love with ideas, and you can fall in love with people. It's a very subjective experience. And I'm loyal to that experience.

Sharing a triumph with someone you love is an incredible high.

What love is to man, music is to the arts and to mankind.

Love is not the dying moan of a distant violin - it's the triumphant twang of a bedspring.

To fall in love is awfully simple, but to fall out of love is simply awful.

When we're children we're told love is going to be great: Just fall in love, the rest will take care of itself - and then we fall in love and we realize, Okay, this is actually really, really hard work. This guy doesn't just tell me I'm great every day, you know?

Christianity taught men that love is worth more than intelligence.

Yeah, exactly, you can talk about politics in music, you can talk about something else, but that's always going to change, and love is never going to change.

But I still read Shaw on a regular basis. What I love is the nakedness of the polemic and the irresistible good humour. For me, 'Major Barbara' is the greatest of all the plays in that it starts from the rational and proceeds to the ecstatic in a spectacular way, and leaves you very confused if you cling to Euclidean logic.

It's not the size of the house. It's how much love is inside.

Love is an obsessive delusion that is cured by marriage.

Love is based on imagination.

The kind of acting I love is when you watch and you discover what you think perhaps you weren't supposed to see: the chink in the armor.

My life is brillant, My love is pure.

Personally, love is very important for me. There are lots of ordinary things in life, so love should be extraordinary. I hope I achieve that.

Love is just chemistry.

The one who will be found in trial capable of great acts of love is ever the one who is always doing considerate small ones.

Unrequited love is always a great thing.

Both of my books, 'Love Is a Mix Tape' and 'Talking to Girls About Duran Duran,' are about how music gets tangled up with all our other emotional memories. Since I'm an obsessive music fan, I'm always seeking out new sonic thrills.

Expiring for love is beautiful but stupid.

I think love is the through line and it's universal and it doesn't matter what period of time, time or place, or people, that's something we all connect to. That's the thin thread that I think keeps it altogether.

In cases where every thing is understood, and measured, and reduced to rule, love is out of the question.

'Love' is so short of perfect rhymes that convention allows half-rhymes like 'move.' The alternative is a plague of doves, or a kind of poem in which the poet addresses his adored both as 'love' and as 'guv' - a perfectly decent solution once, but only once, in a while.

What I love is a peanut butter and pickle sandwich. I'll just have peanut butter and bananas, then peanut butter and pickles. Peanut butter and chocolate I don't recommend.

It's incredibly stressful when the person you love is having a child.

One hour of right-down love is worth an age of dully living on.

Love is really my nemesis. I never really allowed myself to indulge in such basic things because I was so motivated and thought that if I did I wouldn't succeed.

Love is the one thing in life that makes everything worthwhile.

Love is the one thing in life that makes everything worthwhile.

———❧⟡❧———

Picking and choosing what kind of love is worth recognizing is an expensive choice. Is discrimination worth that price?

———❧⟡❧———

To love is to believe, to hope, to know; Tis an essay, a taste of Heaven below!

———❧⟡❧———

I'm human, I feel, I understand. That's the highest level of love, is understanding - when you can understand someone, when you can love them with their flaws and their faults. So I understand, I consider. I may speak the truth, but I'll consider your feelings, too.

———❧⟡❧———

I really love jazz, but I will never be a jazz musician as much as I dream. But, I think that the jazz music I love is there in my music.

———❧⟡❧———

For love is a willful stirring of our thoughts unto God, so that it receive nothing that is against the love of Jesus Christ, and therewith that it be lasting in sweetness of devotion; and that is the perfection of this life.

All love is original, no matter how many other people have loved before.

I think teen-age love is a great thing. There's nothing quite like it and never will be for the rest of your life.

I love listening to songs that are from the heart and that touch the heart. So, love is the preferred theme for most of the songs that I sing.

Courtney Love is really cool and funny. I would like to meet Julia Roberts and Cameron Diaz. I think I could play their daughters.

For love that time was not as love is nowadays.

My great love is my home county of Cornwall, I love to sit and watch people enjoying themselves on the beaches and in the harbour towns of Cornwall.

Nobody can take what I love away from me. I would like to believe that love is the only energy I've ever used as a writer. I've never written out of anger, although anger has informed love.

Cooking is great, love is grand, but souffles fall and lovers come and go. But you can always depend on a book!

Every woman in her late 20s goes through a period where she just doesn't believe love is out there anymore, but it is. And I think the minute you stop looking for it is when it comes for you.

The song Venus de Milo, the whole subject of it is Love is a drug.

I've never cared for the idea of a career path, or where a film might 'take me.' My love is for acting not money, so I only take on roles that I find challenging, in stories I find interesting.

———⬥⬥⬥———

Genuine freedom is possible only where there is genuine love. And genuine love is not possible without truth.

———⬥⬥⬥———

Love is an obsession. It has that quality to it. But there are healthy obsessions, and mine is one of them.

———⬥⬥⬥———

There are aspects of love that I once undervalued. Kindness. Having a sort of honor when love is on the table.

———⬥⬥⬥———

Working a job I love is mentally less stressful than punching in a clock everyday, but it's a lot busier.

———⬥⬥⬥———

Love is a big thing - it's part of who you become, how you grow up. I had a wonderful husband, and I'm very lucky I have a second wonderful husband. You know, some people don't even score the first time.

———◆※◆———

All of my free time is made up of motor sports endeavors, be them motorcycles or off-road racing or track days. I just love anything with an engine. That is one of my main loves. Obviously, my other well-known love is Kristen Bell.

———◆※◆———

In mine opinion, love is fitter than fear, gentleness better than beating, to bring up a child rightly in learning.

———◆※◆———

Love is the true means by which the world is enjoyed: our love to others, and others love to us.

———◆※◆———

Love is the reason you were born.

———◆※◆———

Someone asked me a while back, 'Why do artists always write about love?' And I was like, 'Love is the coolest thing that's ever happened in the world.'

I believe that love is the choice we make to raise ourselves and others to the highest planes of existence.

For what the lover would, that would the beloved; what she would ask of him that should he go before to grant. Without accord such as this, love is but a bond and a constraint.

My first love is the sport, and it will always be my priority.

Love is a big word. I believe in Love. I believe that God is Love.

Imagination which comes into play in falling in love is different from any other. Certainly in my case, and I've fallen in love all my life, one imagines the person to be as you want them to be. They frequently turn out to be someone different, for better or worse.

When you're a writer, you pull your life into your work. My first love is cinema. That's where I want to be judged.

———◦❦◦———

The film Punch - Drunk Love is how you see the world when you're in love. You don't see somebody's psychological baggage necessarily, you see the person walking out of the light.

———◦❦◦———

I fall in love with contradictions without understanding. I can't really portray them unless I do. So in a roundabout way I have to fall in love, it's my duty. If love is about understanding and understanding is compassion and compassion is love, I have to have compassion towards the world.

———◦❦◦———

I find love stories satisfying when you can see the work - when you can really watch people find each other and fall in love, a little bit at a time. I like slow burns. Falling in love is so good; why would you want to rush it?

———◦❦◦———

I believe in the power of song. Under the spell of the right song, passion is within reach, love is close by, and you are not alone!

For me, love is the most important force. It moves the universe.

Love is to be nurtured, protected, and respected, and entered into with a clear mind and a sound heart.

Love is a quicksilver word; though you see plainly where it is, you have only to put your finger on it to find that it is not there but someplace else.

There are different definitions of love, and one of the most wonderful definitions of love is to allow somebody to be.

Love is easy! Kindness is easy. So I try on my Twitter page to acknowledge everyone that reaches out to me. I try to make my page - I can't control the rest of Twitter - but I try to make my page a safe place for people.

For a boy or girl, driving cars that they love is fun.

At the risk of sounding hopelessly romantic, love is the key element. I really love to play with different musicians who come from different cultural backgrounds.

Under the spell of the right song, passion is within reach... love is close by... and you are not alone! With such potency, music should be treated with care. The sound, the feel, the presentation... everything! It is a medicine. It is a teacher!

I've been writing a lot about my encounter with love. Which is the white stag as far as songwriting is concerned because love songs are so banal, and my experience with love is anything but that.

If you just stop and think, baby, honey, love is a funny thing. Whatever you put in, that's what you expect to gain.

What's the difference between male and female passion? If love is a drug, what are its side effects? Rhye makes chill-out music, but it never quite lets your mind switch off.

A film that I love is 'Deliverance' from back in the day. You start out with these archetypal characters - the hero, the bookworm, the pacifist - and by the end, it's all turned upside down. I love that.

What I love - and I'm a journalist - and what I love is finding hidden patterns; I love being a data detective.

Love is sweeping the country.

The guy I read and I love is Irvin Yalom.

Our family is very tight. Just like any family, we have our ups and downs, but the love is always going to be there. I try to go to my parents' house as much as I can.

Just being able to get paid to do something you love is a wonderful thing. That said, a writer's daily routine, unless you're Dominick Dunne, isn't exactly glamorous. Much of it amounts to drudgery, staring at a computer screen all day in a room by yourself, juggling nouns and verbs to make a demanding editor happy.

To see two couples that are battling to make it work just shows that love is in a marriage, but there are also trials and things that you have to make it through and showing women and men how to keep it spicy.

Love is all fun and games until someone loses an eye or gets pregnant.

I mean, there's times to rock and roll, and I love that too. But I think my first love is acoustic music.

Love is the big booming beat which covers up
the noise of hate.

I wonder if most people ever ask themselves
why love is connected with reproduction.
And if they do ask themselves about this, I
wonder what answer they give.

It's a misconception that love can only foster
between two people of opposite sex. Love is a
bond.

The most valuable insight on choosing whom
to love is to be honest with yourself about the
man standing before you.

Love is agony, isn't it? I've been involved with
someone for some time now, but it's all so
complicated. It's never straightforward is it?
You meet someone, you fall in love, it's the
most wonderful thing ever but... There's
always something that's not quite right about
love, isn't there?

All of the art that I love is about peeling back
layers and delving into something that's in a
subconscious or dream realm. People like Jan
Svankmajer, or the artist Yoshimoto Nara, or
David Lynch.

To make a living from doing something I love
is fantastic. As long as people want to listen to
me, I'll keep doing it. In fact, to tell you the
truth, even if no one did want to listen to me,
I'd still be doing it!

My Catholic faith is my life. Any artist, if he is
to be faithful to how he perceives the world
and to the nature of his creative gifts, cannot
divorce the two. To create is to love. To love is
to create.

I consider myself very lucky. I'm known for
photographing celebrities, but, in a nutshell,
my first love is photography.

Love is not altogether a delirium, yet it has
many points in common therewith.

What Tolstoy is on about is that carnal love is not a good idea.

All love is unrequited. All of it.

Love is - OK, it's 20 things, but it isn't 19. And I think that love reaches for something which is very, very deep in us and is very easily obscured, and is also very easily denied, which is the instinct towards the other person, other than toward the self.

God is what keeps us together after the love is gone.

Love is by far bigger than the government can ever be.

Love is the beginning, the middle, and the end of the pathway of discipleship. It comforts, counsels, cures, and consoles.

Love is more than one thing.

I think I understand passion. Love is something else.

Love is bigger than government.

Love is something that grows, that comes from nourishment; it builds.

Music is where my love is. I don't think the acting thing is going to start outweighing that, but I think it's going to start being a good chunk of something I want to do.

Love is hard.

Love is not love until love's vulnerable.

Austin is such a free and creative place, but I can't enjoy it as much because everyone I love is back in L.A.

I learned what I really love is making films, not the film business. I want to be on the set, meeting with writers, I want that freedom. I love it now.

Love is what sometimes holds us and binds us when we're not so happy.

Romantic love is painful.

Well, for me, what I've learned at the very end of this, love is sharing, and I think that really is, for me, the best place to go to experience love, is sharing.

That will to love is very powerful. But it doesn't always win.

Love to me, God, this is so difficult... To me, love is when you meet that person and you think, 'This is it, this is who I'm supposed to be with.'

Oh, well, my first love is comedy or singing and dancing.

———◦◦◦———

Love is great, but not as a password.

———◦◦◦———

All the things I love is what my business is all about.

———◦◦◦———

For me, love is happiness and inspiration.

———◦◦◦———

The most dire disaster in love is the death of imagination.

———◦◦◦———

People say they love truth, but in reality they want to believe that which they love is true.

———◦◦◦———

I've been in a lot of fiery relationships, and it is so exciting. But there's a more profound feeling when the love is just real and not so painful.

———✦◦❃◦✦———

Love is like nothing else on this earth, but only when it is shared with someone wonderful like you.

———✦◦❃◦✦———

Love is a mess, at best, and I figure it can be very real in spite of all the things people try to attach to it.

———✦◦❃◦✦———

There aren't really many compliments flying around with me and my friends. It's a lot of tough love. But you know, that love is there, and if you need to have a serious conversation, you just gotta wait for the right time to do it.

———✦◦❃◦✦———

Sex is funny and love is serious.

———✦◦❃◦✦———

'Which is stronger, politics or love?' is like asking, 'Which is stronger, exhaling or inhaling?' They are two sides of the same thing.

———◆◆◆———

Love is not a union merely between two creatures, it is a union between two spirits.

———◆◆◆———

Love is an emotion. It can't be seen or touched, and it is experienced differently by everyone, therefore it is difficult to measure.

———◆◆◆———

Love is the eternal quest: almost everyone wants to love and be loved.

———◆◆◆———

For you to ask advice on the rules of love is no better than to ask advice on the rules of madness.

———◆◆◆———

If someone explains me the definition of love, I will give my life to the person. Love is a thing which is difficult to understand. Love is always evolving.

———◆◆◆———

Love is a passion that hath friends in the garrison.

Love is the terrible secret people are suspected of unless they're married, then one always suspects they don't.

I can only know what love is insofar as I can feel it.

Love is everywhere.

Love is such that God grants us one person who we can spend the rest of our life with. It rarely happens that we don't.

Courtney Love is a loose cannon. She says what she thinks. She's wild on the red carpet. You get the best sound bites from Courtney Love.

I believe 'love' is very nice to hear, but it's used so much that it's come to a point where it's almost meaningless.

———◦✦◦———

If it wasn't for music, I would think that love is mortal.

———◦✦◦———

Love is messy. It's not something that's real clean.

———◦✦◦———

I think love is a huge factor in fiction and in real life. Is there a risk? Always. In fiction and in life.

———◦✦◦———

Well, love is confusing at all ages, but especially when you're 17.

———◦✦◦———

When you have children love is always there in the best form.

———◦✦◦———

My first love is acting on stage. A sitcom is a hybrid of stage and film.

Love is a gift.

I love no woman, for love is a serious business, not a jest.

Love is a peculiar thing.

I sometimes think love is God's way of hoodwinking people into having kids. You fall in love, and all that passion goes into procreating and wanting children.

Dance music is my love, is my passion, is my life. I live for my fans and take my art very seriously.

Why not hold on to whatever I've got because it's as good as it's ever going to get. How can I believe that love is coming, how can I even believe that love exists; if I don't believe it's spiritually based?

It doesn't matter if a child comes to you or through you. That love is still the same. You are still a mother.

I'm still kinda old-school. We're twittering, and we're all twitterers. And we write tweets. The only thing I don't love is twits.

'Hell is for Children' is amazing to do every night and 'Promises in the Dark' and 'Love Is a Battlefied,' of course, but my absolute favorite would be 'Heartbreaker.' It's the one that started everything, so it has a very special place in my heart. And it still rocks every night! It's so fun to do.

My only hope to receive love is to let you see who I am, then I may believe you.

And that's what I really love, is finding a script and fantasizing and going to a different world and kind of portraying a character that is interesting. Because other lives interest us, that's why we read magazines like 'People' and try and fascinate and drool over what other people are doing.

I like Anastacia's version of Love is Alive best.

All my roots are Broadway. I got my Equity Card doing a Broadway show, and my first love is theater.

My first love is producing.

I have a respect for the 3-D computer-generated action movies, but my first love is stuff like 'Lethal Weapon.'

You don't have to have lots of love affairs to know what love is.

What I love is the writing, it's not having written. I like the process of it.

Love is a beautiful feeling.

Love is such a fleeting emotion. It's such a small part of the things you do in your life.

A film that I love is 'Raising Arizona' and that's funny but it's quite indie and weird and odd and quirky. I'd love to do something like that. Who knows?

I was alone for five years. Having a love is a gigantic bonus in life, but I wasn't unhappy when I was single, either.

When love is deep, much can be accomplished.

No, actually 'The Host' was totally a palate-cleanser for me. I wanted to do something a little bit different than romantic love. Romantic love is in there, obviously, because I enjoy writing about that and living it a lot.

The virtue of Love is nothing and all, or that Nothing visible out of which All Things proceed. Its power is through All Things; its height is as high as God; its greatness is as great as God.

As in all matters involving love, which has so many different meanings, you find that the feeling that we label 'love' is not a simple feeling, it's a very complex one. Under the heading 'love' can come all sorts of rage and desperation.

One of the only TV shows that I really love is 'Twin Peaks.' Kyle McLachlan plays Agent Dale Cooper, and I love Dale Cooper, so I'm in love with Kyle McLachlan. He could be my dad, so it's really weird.

The only instrument I know how to really play, and the instrument that I absolutely love, is the piano. I have been playing piano ever since I have been 9.

I think my love is storytelling. No matter what it is, it's storytelling. And so whatever the medium is, what's right for the story, I enjoy doing it.

I want love, because love is the best feeling in the whole world.

For me, one thing I love is having an arc for a character.

My kind of gay, meeting a woman and falling in love, is a different experience because it wasn't anything about 'Oh, I've always been gay and I'm breaking the chains.'

I've never done anything for money. My first love is things of limited commercial appeal. I could be happy doing Shakespeare for the rest of my life.

Freedom of love is freedom to say yes to many lovers.

Perfect happiness is knowing that everyone I love is healthy, safe, and content.

Spiritual men have taken into their head
something that is to be realized. They have
concepts of love, goodness, and the like,
which they would like to see realized;
therefore they want to set up a kingdom of
love on earth, in which no one any longer acts
from selfishness, but each one 'from love.'
Love is to rule.

———❦❦❦———

I think 'All Out of Love' is my favorite song
because it's been the most successful. It's been
in about 30 movies, it's been a number one
record, and it keeps getting played on the
radio, it's always somewhere.

———❦❦❦———

All love is lost but upon God alone.

———❦❦❦———

What I love is this idea of a wardrobe, the
idea that we're establishing certain signatures
and updating them, that a change in colour or
fabric is enough.

———❦❦❦———

I grew up listening to hits, and if I write
something I feel, I think that's pretty mass
appeal. I'm not very elitist with music. Love is
universal; a great melody is universal; it goes

around the world; it's not just American. A great song can touch the world.

I think at its most mature, love is a very bourgeois state. There is something about luxuriating in the nest of love that people fall into naturally.

On YouTube you can tell what countries are watching and I've definitely noted a strong Australian following. You can plan your tours around where the love is on Twitter and YouTube - before, you couldn't tell.

Love is reaching out to try to get to the other person.

One thing I love is to do children's hospital visits.

Love is the essence of life; love touches all of our work. Love never leaves us. It clings to us, and we cling to it.

What I love is acting, and the technical stuff
does tend to slow things down.

To work with someone you love is something
special, an incredible experience. But it could
be a negative. You have to make a strong
commitment to be honest; you're not just
being polite, like strangers on an airplane;
you're working.

The chemistry of love is something which is
extremely extremely unbelievable. This is
something we have planned for more than
two years, so I hope that we are going to start
in the beginning of next year.

Love is a component of many different things
- the baggage you bring, the moment, what
you need in your life, seeing someone as a
portal for understanding everything, and all
the intensity that brings. It's not something to
count on and act like it's a stable thing.

'Punch-Drunk Love' is my favorite movie.

What I would love is a crossover between 'Royal Pains' and 'Burn Notice,' that we could be involved in some sort of gun play intrigue. I would really love that because we have no guns. We have nowhere near enough explosions and guns on the set.

———⋆⟡⟡⋆———

Love is just such a crucial, wonderful thing, and if you are lucky enough to find somebody who genuinely loves you, grab that person and hold on to that person, and nothing else matters.

———⋆⟡⟡⋆———

Love is of that excellent nature, that it is esteemed by the best of men, and accepted from the meanest persons; what then is the affection of a Father!

———⋆⟡⟡⋆———

Love is important. I didn't have the energy to be giving it to somebody else in a way that they deserved, and I knew that. So I've always been scared to go too far with somebody I care for because I knew there would come a day when I'd need to pick up and finish a painting for the next three months. That day is inevitable.

———⋆⟡⟡⋆———

When you're younger, you have ideas and visions of what you're going to be like when you're older and what love is going to be like and who you're gonna be married to and all of these different things.

———⊰❦⊱———

I think love is blind. I hate to use that cliched statement, but people, when they love somebody, they seem to be able to somehow to put aside red flags.

———⊰❦⊱———

I would definitely like to continue playing Aquaman. Playing a superhero is a lot of fun. Creating these stories is a lot of fun. I do what I love. And what I love is entertaining people.

———⊰❦⊱———

What I do love is the traveling... and getting paid for it! I like being in front of a camera... It's an outlet. It's fun! If you look through my photo album, they are all modeling poses. My mom was a young mom, so she took tons of pictures of me.

———⊰❦⊱———

Regardless of who you are or who you like, love is love.

I'll go my way by myself, love is only a dance.

We define ourselves, in part, by the discriminations we make. The value of what we love is enriched by our understanding of what we dislike.

Love is... never asking for more than you are prepared to give.

MORE

Check out the website for more cool stuff

www.connorfun.com

www.ingramcontent.com/pod-product-compliance
Lightning Source LLC
Chambersburg PA
CBHW071405280526
45787CB00001B/445